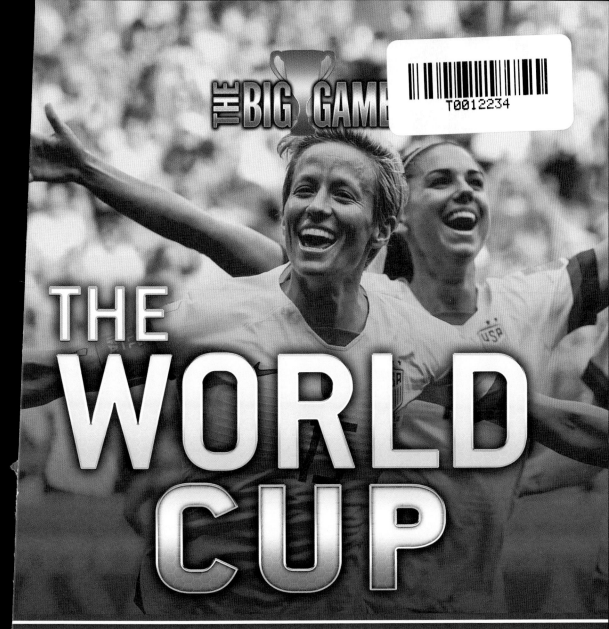

THE BIG GAME

THE WORLD CUP

SOCCER'S GREATEST TOURNAMENT

Matt Scheff

Lerner Publications ◆ Minneapolis

Lerner Publications Company
An imprint of Lerner Publishing Group, Inc.
241 First Avenue North
Minneapolis, MN 55401 USA

For reading levels and more information, look up this title at www.lernerbooks.com.

Main body text set in Conduit ITC Std.
Typeface provided by International Typeface Corp.

Editor: Alison Lorenz **Designer:** Viet Chu

Library of Congress Cataloging-in-Publication Data

Names: Scheff, Matt, author.
Title: The World Cup : soccer's greatest tournament / Matt Scheff.
Description: Minneapolis : Lerner Publications, 2021 | Series: The big game (Lerner sports) | Includes bibliographical references and index. | Audience: Ages 7–11 | Audience: Grades K–1 | Summary: "An exploration of the history, amazing moments, and greatest players of the women's and men's soccer World Cup" — Provided by publisher.
Identifiers: LCCN 2019039962 (print) | LCCN 2019039963 (ebook) | ISBN 9781541597563 (library binding) | ISBN 9781728401270 (ebook)
Subjects: LCSH: World Cup (Soccer)—History—Juvenile literature. | Soccer players—Juvenile literature. | Women soccer players—Juvenile literature. | Soccer—History—Juvenile literature.
Classification: LCC GV943.49 .S32 2021 | (print) | LCC GV943.49 | (ebook) | DDC 796.334/668—dc23

LC record available at https://lccn.loc.gov/2019039962
LC ebook record available at https://lccn.loc.gov/2019039963

Manufactured in the United States of America
1-47860-48300-1/27/2020

Contents

Megan Rapinoe runs with the ball during the 2019 Women's World Cup Final.

Claiming the Cup

Megan Rapinoe stared down goalkeeper Sari van Veenendaal in the 2019 Women's World Cup Final. The crowd roared as the US star prepared to take a penalty kick. It was the game's second half, and neither the US nor the Netherlands had scored yet. This kick could give the US the lead.

Rapinoe made her move. She drilled a hard, low shot toward the right side of the goal. The blast froze van Veenendaal, and the ball zipped into the net. Rapinoe struck her famous pose, her arms spread wide as her teammates celebrated.

The US women's team had one of the most dominant World Cup performances in history. It was one of many memorable moments to come from soccer's biggest stage.

Facts at a Glance

- More than 90,000 fans packed the Rose Bowl to watch the 1999 Women's World Cup Final. It was the largest crowd ever to attend a women's sporting event.

- England was knocked out of the 2015 Women's World Cup when one of its players accidentally scored on her own goal.

- Marta holds the all-time women's record for goals scored during the World Cup with 17. Miroslav Klose holds the men's record with 16.

- In 1966, the Jules Rimet Trophy, the trophy awarded to World Cup winners at the time, was stolen. A dog named Pickles found it hidden in a bush.

Uruguay's men's team in 1930,
when they won the first World Cup

CHAPTER 1

THE WORLD CUP

IN THE EARLY 20TH CENTURY, THE POPULARITY OF SOCCER
exploded across the world. The Fédération Internationale
de Football Association (FIFA) set the rules for the
international game. But FIFA lacked a major worldwide event.
In 1928, FIFA president Jules Rimet imagined a tournament
that would settle a huge question: Which nation had the best
soccer players?

THE EARLY DAYS

Rimet created the World Cup tournament. But it wasn't a hit right away. Only 13 national teams traveled to Uruguay for the first World Cup in 1930. The host nation defeated Argentina to become the first World Cup champions.

War and politics interrupted the World Cup for its first two decades. But the tournament continued to grow. Players such as Ferenc Puskás, Pelé, and Diego Maradona became global celebrities. About 3.5 billion people watched at least some of the 2018 World Cup. That's almost half the world's population!

Belgium's Nicholas Hoydonck (*left*) fights the US's Bertram Patenaude during the 1930 World Cup.

THE WOMEN'S WORLD CUP

The Women's World Cup began in 1991. The United States and the Netherlands clashed in the tournament's first final. With just two minutes left, Michelle Akers-Stahl of the United States scored a goal. The United States won a 2–1 victory and became the first Women's World Cup champions.

Michelle Akers-Stahl [*right*] celebrates with her teammates after the US's 1991 victory.

In 1999, more than 90,000 fans packed the Rose Bowl in Pasadena, California, for the Women's World Cup Final. It was the largest crowd ever to attend a women's sporting event. The US women won again, this time defeating China in a thrilling shootout.

The game has only grown since then. Stars such as Marta, Abby Wambach, and Megan Rapinoe push the competition to higher levels, thrilling fans around the world.

Mia Hamm of the US women's team in 1999

Inside the Game

Soccer is often a low-scoring sport. But when the US women faced Thailand in 2019, they dominated with a 13–0 victory. No men's or women's team has ever scored more goals in a World Cup game.

Max Morlock (*left*) slides to score Germany's first goal in the 1954 World Cup Final.

CHAPTER 2

MEMORABLE MOMENTS

FOR ALMOST A CENTURY, THE WORLD CUP HAS GIVEN fans moments they'll never forget. From stirring comebacks to heart-pounding finishes, here are some of the greatest moments in World Cup history.

The 1954 World Cup Final in Bern, Switzerland, was a mismatch. Hungary was the best team in the world. They had Ferenc Puskás, the game's best player. West Germany was a team of part-time players.

Hungary scored two goals in the first eight minutes. But as rain soaked the field, the pace of play slowed. West Germany took advantage, scoring two goals to tie the game. Then, with six minutes left, Helmut Rahn booted in a goal to give West Germany the lead. Hungary couldn't strike back. West Germany walked off with one of the biggest upsets in World Cup history.

West Germany's Fritz Walter (*right*) takes a shot.

The 1999 Women's World Cup Final was a game for the ages. The US and China played lockdown defense for 90 minutes of regulation and 30 minutes of extra time. Penalty kicks would decide the winner.

The score was tied 4−4. US defender Brandi Chastain had the final attempt. She ran to the ball and booted it with her left foot. The shot sailed into the right corner of the goal, just beyond

Chastain celebrates her goal, and the US World Cup win, in 1999.

Chastain's teammates swarm her after her winning penalty kick.

the goalkeeper's reach and into the net. Chastain ripped off her jersey and dropped to her knees in one of the most famous celebrations in sports history.

It was the opening game of the 1990 World Cup. Argentina was at the top of the soccer world and a favorite to win it all.

Cameroon knew they were facing long odds. They decided to surprise Argentina with hard physical play. The strategy worked. Cameroon took the lead with a goal in the 67th minute. A pair of red cards left the team down two players. But even playing nine on 11, they held off Argentina to close out a stunning victory.

Cameroon's Roger Feutmba blows past two Argentinian players at the 1990 World Cup.

Cameroon's Victor Ndip Akem slides into Argentina's Diego Maradona.

A CRUSHING MISTAKE

England was on a mission to make its first Women's World Cup Final in 2015. The team cruised through the early rounds before facing Japan in the semifinals.

The score was tied 1–1 in the final minutes. Japan pushed the ball toward England's goal. Then a long pass came up short. England's Laura Bassett tried to clear the ball by kicking it out of bounds. Instead, Bassett's attempt sailed through the air and into her own goal! The mistake proved to be the game winner for Japan, and England suffered a painful defeat.

England goalie Karen Bardsley tries to block Bassett's ball.

Bassett's own goal meant that Japan advanced to face the US in the final.

Inside the Game

Like quick action? So does Turkey's Hakan Sükür. When Turkey faced South Korea in 2002, Sükür scored a goal just 10.89 seconds after kickoff. It's the fastest goal scored in World Cup history.

The US's Abby Wambach celebrates her team's World Cup victory over Japan in 2015.

CHAPTER 3

CLUTCH PERFORMERS

SOCCER IS A TEAM SPORT. BUT ONE PLAYER CAN CHANGE the game. Read on to meet some of the greatest performers in World Cup history, and learn how they helped propel their teams to victory.

PELÉ

Pelé was one of soccer's first true superstars. He was quick, powerful, and dangerous with the ball. Pelé burst onto the World Cup scene in 1958. He played in four World Cups, helping Brazil win three of them. His 12 World Cup goals rank fifth on the all-time list.

MIA HAMM

Mia Hamm helped the Women's World Cup become a huge international event. Hamm played on the US team that won the first World Cup in 1991. She and her teammates won it all again eight years later. Hamm scored eight goals in her World Cups and became a soccer legend.

MIROSLAV KLOSE

No man has scored more during the World Cup than Germany's Miroslav Klose has scored. Klose used his huge leaps and powerful strikes to score 16 World Cup goals. His greatest moment came in 2014, when he helped Germany win the World Cup.

MARTA

Many fans consider Brazil's Marta to be the greatest female soccer player of all time. She is lightning-quick with amazing ball skills. Marta played in five Women's World Cups for Brazil. She scored 17 World Cup goals, more than any player in history has scored.

RONALDO

Ronaldo was a scoring machine. The Brazilian superstar was always on the attack. His power, speed, and skill made him almost impossible to stop. Ronaldo's greatest World Cup performance came in 2002. He scored eight goals and led Brazil to the championship. His 15 career World Cup goals are the second most ever scored by one player.

MEGAN RAPINOE

The US women dominated the 2019 World Cup, and no player was more clutch than Megan Rapinoe was. With six goals, Rapinoe won the Golden Boot as the tournament's leading scorer. Her pink hair, fearless style, and trademark celebrations helped make her a huge star.

DIEGO MARADONA

Diego Maradona of Argentina was a wizard with the soccer ball. He was quick, accurate, and creative. His greatest moment came at the 1986 World Cup. Maradona weaved 60 yards through a sea of defenders before scoring what fans called the Goal of the Century.

Abby Wambach

Abby Wambach's 14 career World Cup goals tie her for second most among women players. Wambach was famous for scoring with her head. But she was just as dangerous with her feet. She played in four World Cups, helping the United States win it all in 2015.

French fans cheer during the 2019 Women's World Cup

CHAPTER 4

WORLD CUP CULTURE

THE WORLD CUP IS ONE OF THE BIGGEST SPORTING events in the world. Each tournament takes on the flavor of its host city. Fans and players take in the local culture, food, and sights. They crowd into packed stadiums, party together in the streets, and celebrate the game they love. Millions more watch the games on television and social media. Reporters cover the competition from every angle.

In the Stadium

A World Cup match is a spectacle. Fans wearing their team's colors pack the stands. They wave flags and start booming chants and songs. On the pitch, the focus stays on the game. No band or performer plays at halftime. Instead, players take a 15-minute rest while groundskeepers quickly repair the turf.

When the final minute of the final game has ticked away, the winners accept their trophy. Men's teams used to receive the Jules Rimet Trophy under one condition. If a team won the trophy three times, they kept it permanently—which the Brazilian team did, in 1970. Since then, men's teams compete for the FIFA World Cup Trophy. Women's teams take home the FIFA Women's World Cup Trophy.

US fans often paint their faces with the American flag.

Fans of the winning team celebrate with parades, songs, and parties. When the action is over, fans and players head home. By that time, the next host city is already preparing for one of the biggest sporting events in the world.

The US women's team won their fourth championship at the 2019 Women's World Cup.

Inside the Game

The Jules Rimet Trophy was hidden in a shoebox during World War II (1939–1945). In 1966, the trophy was stolen in England. A dog named Pickles later found it hidden in a bush. In 1983, the trophy went missing again. Officials believe thieves melted it down for its gold.

French fans celebrate the country's 2018 World Cup victory near the Arc de Triomphe in Paris.

World Cup

Year	Winner
1930	Uruguay
1934	Italy
1938	Italy
1950	Uruguay
1954	West Germany
1958	Brazil
1962	Brazil
1966	England
1970	Brazil
1974	West Germany
1978	Argentina
1982	Italy
1986	Argentina
1990	West Germany
1994	Brazil
1998	France
2002	Brazil
2006	Italy
2010	Spain
2014	Germany
2018	France

Women's World Cup

Year	Winner
1991	USA
1995	Norway
1999	USA
2003	Germany
2007	Germany
2011	Japan
2015	USA
2019	USA

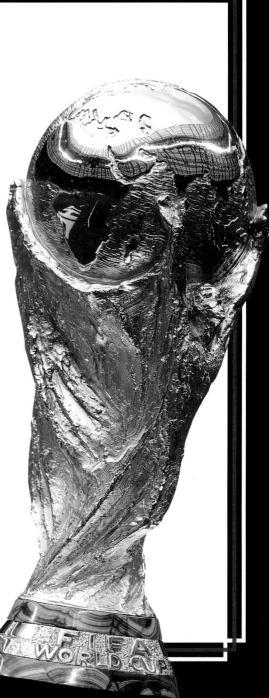

Glossary

clutch: having the ability to perform at one's best in high-pressure situations

extra time: 30 minutes of time added to games after regulation time and injury time have ended

Golden Boot: the trophy awarded to the top goal-scorer in each World Cup

international: involving two or more nations

penalty kick: an uncontested kick taken after the opposing team commits a foul

pitch: a soccer field

regulation: 90 minutes, the standard length of time of a soccer game

social media: websites and apps that allow users to generate content

spectacle: a large, impressive public display

upset: a match won unexpectedly by the underdog team

Further Information

FIFA Women's World Cup
https://www.fifa.com/womensworldcup/

FIFA World Cup
https://www.fifa.com/worldcup/

Luke, Andrew. *U.S. Women's Team*. Broomall, PA: Mason Crest, 2019.

Morey, Allan. *The World Cup*. Minneapolis: Bellwether Media, 2019.

Moussavi, Sam. *World Cup Heroes*. Minneapolis: Abdo, 2019.

Sports Illustrated Kids
https://www.sikids.com/

Index

Photo Acknowledgments

Image credits: zhengshun tangGetty Images, pp. 2, 3, Marcio Machado/Getty Images, p. 4; Lionel Bonaventure/AFP/Getty Images, pp. 5, 25; Hulton Picture Library/ALLSPORT/Getty Images, p. 6; Popperfoto/Getty Images, pp. 7, 10; Tommy Cheng/AFP/Getty Images, p. 8; David Madison/Getty Images, p. 9; Keystone-France/Gamma-Keystone/Getty Images, p. 11; Roberto Schmidt/AFP/Getty Images, p. 12; Jed Jacobsohn/Getty Images, p. 13; Bob Thomas Sports Photography/Getty Images, p. 14; Peter Robinson - PA Images/Getty Images, p. 15; Ronald Martinez/Getty Images, p. 16; Mike Hewitt/FIFA/Getty Images, p. 17; Dennis Grombkowski/Getty Images, pp. 18, 23; Art Rickerby/The LIFE Picture Collection/Getty Images, p. 19; Jonathan Ferrey/Getty Images, p. 20; Sandra Behne/Bongarts/Getty Images, p. 20; Daniela Porcelli/Getty Images, p. 21; Andreas Rentz/Bongarts/Getty Images, p. 21; Robert Cianflone/Getty Images, p. 22; Steve Powell/Allsport/Getty Images, p. 22; Franck Fife/AFP/Getty Images, p. 24; Naomi Baker/FIFA/Getty Images, p. 26; Dave Winter/Icon Sport/Getty Images, p. 27; Molly Darlington-AMA/Getty Images, p. 28; Chris Brunskill/Fantasista/Getty Images, p. 29.

Cover: Philippe Desmazes/Getty Images.